Walter the Educator's
Cooking College

Walter the Educator's Cooking College

A Little Cookbook of the Best Appetizer Recipes

Walter the Educator

SKB

Silent King Books

dedicated to the people that love good food

This book belongs to Walter the Educator's Cooking College Cookbook Series

CONTENTS █

CONTENTS

CONTENTS

CONTENTS

One

Caprese Skewers

Ingredients:

Cherry tomatoes
Fresh Mozzarella balls
Fresh basil leaves
Balsamic glaze
Salt and pepper
Skewers
Instructions:

Rinse the cherry tomatoes and basil leaves.

Skewer one cherry tomato, one fresh Mozzarella ball, and one basil leaf onto each skewer.

Repeat until all ingredients are used.

Sprinkle with salt and pepper.

Drizzle with balsamic glaze.

Serve and enjoy!

This Caprese Skewers recipe is a quick and easy appetizer

that is perfect for any occasion. The combination of fresh Mozzarella, cherry tomatoes, and basil creates a delicious and refreshing flavor. The balsamic glaze adds a tangy and sweet touch that perfectly complements the other ingredients. This recipe is sure to be a crowd-pleaser!

Two

Tomato Bruschetta

Ingredients:

1 baguette, sliced
2 cups diced tomatoes
1/4 cup chopped fresh basil
2 cloves garlic, minced
1/4 cup olive oil
1/4 teaspoon salt
1/4 teaspoon black pepper
1/4 cup grated Parmesan cheese
Directions:

Preheat oven to 350 degrees F.

In a bowl, mix together the diced tomatoes, chopped basil, minced garlic, olive oil, salt, and black pepper.

Place the sliced baguette on a baking sheet and brush each slice with olive oil.

Bake the baguette slices in the preheated oven for 5-7 minutes, or until lightly toasted.

Top each baguette slice with the tomato mixture and sprinkle with Parmesan cheese.

Serve and enjoy!

This appetizer is perfect for any occasion, whether it's a party or a casual get-together. The combination of fresh tomatoes, basil, and garlic is sure to impress your guests!

Three

Cream Cheese Stuffed Mushrooms

Ingredients:

18-20 whole mushrooms

1/2 cup cream cheese, softened

1/4 cup grated parmesan cheese

1/4 cup breadcrumbs

1/2 teaspoon garlic powder

1/4 teaspoon salt

1/4 teaspoon black pepper

2 tablespoons chopped fresh parsley

Instructions:

Preheat oven to 375°F (190°C).

Remove stems from mushrooms and chop finely.

In a mixing bowl, combine chopped mushroom stems, cream cheese, parmesan cheese, breadcrumbs, garlic powder, salt, pepper, and parsley. Mix well.

Stuff the mushroom caps with the cream cheese mixture and place on a baking dish.

Bake for 20-25 minutes or until the mushrooms are tender and the filling is golden brown.

Serve hot and enjoy!

These cream cheese stuffed mushrooms are easy to make and a crowd-pleaser at any party or gathering. The creamy filling pairs perfectly with the meatiness of the mushrooms, making it a perfect appetizer for any occasion.

Four

Kielbasa and Sauerkraut Balls

Ingredients:

1/2 pound kielbasa, diced
1 cup sauerkraut, drained and chopped
1/2 cup breadcrumbs
1/4 cup grated parmesan cheese
1 egg
Salt and pepper to taste
Oil for frying
Instructions:

In a mixing bowl, combine the diced kielbasa and chopped sauerkraut.

Add breadcrumbs, grated parmesan cheese, egg, salt, and pepper to the mixing bowl, and stir until well combined.

Shape the mixture into small balls using your hands.

Heat oil in a deep frying pan over medium-high heat.

Fry the balls until they turn golden brown, which should take around 3 minutes.

Once done, remove the balls from the pan and place them on a plate lined with paper towels to remove any excess oil.

Serve hot and enjoy your Kielbasa and Sauerkraut Balls!

This recipe yields 12-15 balls, depending on the size of each ball. You can also experiment by adding different spices and herbs to the mix to suit your taste.

Five

Oregano and Feta Stuffed Mushrooms

Ingredients:

24 medium-sized mushrooms

1/2 cup crumbled feta cheese

1/4 cup breadcrumbs

2 tablespoons chopped fresh oregano

2 cloves garlic, minced

2 tablespoons olive oil

Salt and pepper to taste

Directions:

Preheat oven to 375 degrees F (190 degrees C).

Remove the stems from the mushrooms and set aside. Arrange the mushroom caps on a baking sheet.

In a small bowl, mix together the feta cheese, breadcrumbs, oregano, garlic, salt, and pepper until well combined.

Finely chop the reserved mushroom stems and add them to the mixture.

Stuff each mushroom cap with a generous amount of the mixture and drizzle with olive oil.

Bake for 20-25 minutes, or until the mushrooms are tender and the filling is golden brown.

Serve hot and enjoy.

This appetizer is the perfect combination of earthy mushrooms, tangy feta cheese, and flavorful oregano. It's a great addition to any party or gathering and is sure to impress your guests.

Six

Spicy Cheese and Cracker Bites

Ingredients:

1 sleeve of crackers (such as Ritz or saltine)
1 cup shredded cheddar cheese
1/4 cup mayonnaise
1/4 tsp garlic powder
1/4 tsp paprika
1/4 tsp cayenne pepper
Fresh parsley for garnish
Instructions:

Preheat oven to 350°F (180°C).

In a small bowl, mix together shredded cheddar cheese, mayonnaise, garlic powder, paprika, and cayenne pepper.

Spread a small amount of the cheese mixture on each cracker and place on a baking sheet.

Bake for 5-7 minutes, or until cheese is melted and bubbly.

Garnish with fresh parsley and serve immediately.

This appetizer is perfect for any occasion, from game day to a dinner party. The spicy cheese mixture adds a kick of flavor to the crunchy crackers, making them a crowd-pleaser. Enjoy!

Seven

Chicken Satay Skewers

Ingredients:

1 lb boneless, skinless chicken breast, cut into strips
   1/4 cup soy sauce
   2 tbsp honey
   1 tbsp lime juice
   1 tsp curry powder
   1 garlic clove, minced
   Bamboo skewers, soaked in water for 30 minutes
   Instructions:

Preheat grill or grill pan to medium-high heat.

In a small bowl, whisk together soy sauce, honey, lime juice, curry powder, and garlic.

Thread chicken strips onto skewers.

Brush chicken with the sauce mixture.

Grill chicken skewers for 5-7 minutes on each side, or until cooked through.

Serve with additional sauce on the side.

This savory and sweet appetizer is perfect for any occasion. The chicken is marinated in a flavorful sauce and then grilled to perfection. The skewers make it easy to eat and add a fun touch to any party spread. Enjoy!

Eight

Chicken and Avocado Bruschetta

Ingredients:

1 lb boneless, skinless chicken breast
1 avocado, diced
1 small red onion, diced
2 cloves garlic, minced
1 tbsp olive oil
Salt and pepper to taste
1 baguette, sliced
1/4 cup chopped fresh cilantro
Instructions:

Preheat oven to 400°F.

Season chicken with salt and pepper, then grill or bake until cooked through. Let cool and dice into small pieces.

In a bowl, mix together diced avocado, red onion, garlic, olive oil, salt, and pepper.

Toast baguette slices in the oven until lightly crispy.

Top each slice with a spoonful of the avocado mixture and diced chicken.

Garnish with chopped cilantro and serve immediately.

This appetizer is perfect for any occasion and combines the creamy texture of avocado with savory chicken on a crispy baguette slice. It's easy to make and sure to impress your guests.

Nine

Turkey Bacon-Wrapped Asparagus

Ingredients:

1 pound asparagus, trimmed
    8 slices turkey bacon
    1/4 cup grated parmesan cheese
    1 tablespoon olive oil
    Salt and pepper, to taste
    Instructions:

Preheat oven to 400°F. Line a baking sheet with parchment paper.

Snap off the tough ends of the asparagus. Divide the asparagus into 8 equal portions.

Take a slice of turkey bacon and wrap it around each asparagus spear, leaving the tips exposed. Place on the prepared baking sheet.

Drizzle the olive oil over the asparagus and sprinkle with salt and pepper. Top with grated parmesan cheese.

Bake for 15-20 minutes, or until the bacon is crispy and the asparagus is tender.

Serve immediately and enjoy!

Ten

Marinara and Mozzarella Stuffed Mushrooms

Ingredients:

16 large mushrooms
1 cup of marinara sauce
1 cup of shredded mozzarella cheese
1/2 cup of breadcrumbs
1/4 cup of grated Parmesan cheese
1 tablespoon of olive oil
Salt and pepper to taste
Fresh basil leaves for garnish
Instructions:

Preheat the oven to 375°F. Line a baking sheet with parchment paper.

Remove the stems from the mushrooms and clean them with

a damp cloth. Place the mushrooms on the prepared baking sheet.

In a small bowl, mix together the breadcrumbs, Parmesan cheese, and olive oil. Set aside.

Spoon a tablespoon of marinara sauce into each mushroom cap.

Sprinkle the shredded mozzarella cheese on top of the marinara sauce.

Sprinkle the breadcrumb mixture over the cheese.

Bake the mushrooms for 20-25 minutes or until the cheese is melted and bubbly.

Garnish with fresh basil leaves and serve hot.

These Marinara and Mozzarella Stuffed Mushrooms are a delicious and easy-to-make appetizer that's perfect for any occasion. The marinara sauce adds a rich and tangy flavor, while the mozzarella cheese provides a creamy and cheesy texture. Serve these mushrooms at your next party or gathering and watch them disappear in minutes!

Eleven

Crabmeat and Avocado Dip

Ingredients:

8 oz. lump crabmeat, drained
2 ripe avocados, peeled and mashed
1/4 cup red onion, finely chopped
1/4 cup red bell pepper, finely chopped
1 jalapeño pepper, seeds removed and finely chopped
1 garlic clove, minced
1/4 cup cilantro, finely chopped
1 lime, juiced
Salt and pepper, to taste
Tortilla chips, for serving
Instructions:

In a medium-sized bowl, combine the mashed avocado, red onion, red bell pepper, jalapeño pepper, garlic, and cilantro.

Gently fold in the crabmeat, being careful not to break it up too much.

Add the lime juice and season with salt and pepper to taste. Cover and refrigerate for at least 30 minutes before serving. Serve with tortilla chips and enjoy!

This dip is perfect for a party or gathering and can be easily doubled or tripled to accommodate larger crowds. It's also a great way to use up any leftover crabmeat you may have from a previous meal.

Twelve

Spinach and Feta Stuffed Phyllo Cups

Ingredients:

1 package of phyllo cups
2 cups fresh spinach, chopped
1/2 cup crumbled feta cheese
1/4 cup chopped onion
1 clove garlic, minced
1/4 cup chopped sundried tomatoes
1 tbsp olive oil
Salt and pepper to taste
Instructions:

Preheat the oven to 350°F.

In a pan, heat the olive oil over medium-high heat. Add the onion and garlic and cook until soft.

Add the chopped spinach and cook until wilted.

Season with salt and pepper to taste.

Remove from heat and let cool for a few minutes.

Add the crumbled feta cheese and chopped sundried tomatoes to the pan and mix well.

Fill each phyllo cup with the spinach and feta mixture.

Bake for 10-12 minutes, or until the phyllo cups are golden brown.

Serve warm and enjoy!

This appetizer is perfect for any gathering, and the combination of spinach and feta cheese is sure to impress your guests.

Thirteen

Seafood Crostini

Ingredients:

1 baguette, sliced into 1/2-inch thick pieces
1/2 pound cooked shrimp, chopped
1/2 pound cooked crabmeat, shredded
1/4 cup mayonnaise
2 tablespoons sour cream
1 tablespoon chopped fresh parsley
1 tablespoon chopped green onion
1 teaspoon lemon zest
Salt and pepper to taste
Olive oil for brushing
Steps:

Preheat the oven to 400°F.

Arrange the baguette slices on a baking sheet and brush with olive oil.

Bake the baguette slices for 5-7 minutes or until lightly toasted.

In a medium bowl, mix together the cooked shrimp, crab-meat, mayonnaise, sour cream, parsley, green onion, lemon zest, salt, and pepper.

Spoon the seafood mixture onto the toasted baguette slices.

Place the crostini back in the oven and bake for an additional 5-7 minutes until heated through.

Serve warm and enjoy your delicious seafood crostini appetizer!

Fourteen

Jalapeno Popper Dip

Ingredients:

8 oz. cream cheese, softened

1/2 cup sour cream

1/2 cup mayonnaise

1 cup shredded cheddar cheese

1/2 cup grated Parmesan cheese

4-5 jalapenos, seeded and chopped

1/2 cup panko breadcrumbs

2 tbsp. butter, melted

Tortilla chips or crackers, for serving

Directions:

Preheat the oven to 375°F.

In a mixing bowl, combine the cream cheese, sour cream, and mayonnaise until smooth.

Stir in the cheddar cheese, Parmesan cheese, and chopped jalapenos.

Transfer the mixture to a 9-inch baking dish.

In a separate bowl, mix the panko breadcrumbs and melted butter until well combined.

Sprinkle the breadcrumb mixture over the top of the dip.

Bake for 25-30 minutes, or until the dip is bubbly and the top is golden brown.

Serve with tortilla chips or crackers.

Enjoy this creamy and spicy Jalapeno Popper Dip with your friends and family!

Fifteen

Bacon-Wrapped Dates with Goat Cheese

Ingredients:

24 pitted dates
8 slices of bacon, cut into thirds
4 oz goat cheese
1 tbsp honey
1 tsp fresh rosemary, chopped
Toothpicks
Instructions:

Preheat oven to 375°F (190°C).

In a small bowl, mix together the goat cheese, honey, and rosemary until well combined.

Stuff each date with a small amount of the goat cheese mixture.

Wrap each stuffed date with a slice of bacon and secure with a toothpick.

Place the bacon-wrapped dates on a parchment-lined baking sheet.

Bake for 15-20 minutes, or until the bacon is crispy and the goat cheese is melted.

Serve warm and enjoy!

This appetizer is perfect for any party or gathering and is sure to be a hit with bacon lovers. The sweetness of the dates pairs perfectly with the salty bacon and tangy goat cheese. Give it a try and impress your guests with this unique and delicious appetizer!

Sixteen

Bell Pepper and Feta
Cheese Bites

Ingredients:

2 bell peppers (any color)
   4 oz feta cheese
   1/4 cup chopped fresh parsley
   2 tbsp lemon juice
   1 tbsp olive oil
   Salt and pepper to taste
   Toothpicks
   Instructions:

Preheat oven to 375°F.

Cut the bell peppers into bite-sized pieces, making sure to remove the seeds and membranes.

In a small bowl, crumble the feta cheese and mix with parsley, lemon juice, olive oil, salt, and pepper.

Stuff each bell pepper piece with the feta cheese mixture.

Place the stuffed bell pepper pieces on a baking sheet and bake for 12-15 minutes, or until the cheese is melted and bubbly.

Remove from the oven and let cool for a few minutes before inserting a toothpick into each piece.

Serve warm and enjoy!

This recipe is a great way to showcase the sweetness and crunchiness of bell peppers. The combination of feta cheese, parsley, and lemon juice gives the bites a tangy and refreshing flavor that will leave your guests wanting more.

Seventeen

Pepper Jack Cheese
Jalapeno Poppers

Ingredients:

8 jalapeno peppers
4 ounces pepper jack cheese, shredded
4 ounces cream cheese, softened
1/4 teaspoon garlic powder
1/4 teaspoon onion powder
1/4 teaspoon cumin
1/4 teaspoon chili powder
Salt and black pepper, to taste
1 egg, beaten
1/2 cup panko bread crumbs
Cooking spray
Directions:

Preheat the oven to 400°F. Line a baking sheet with parchment paper and set aside.

Cut off the jalapeno stems and slice the peppers in half lengthwise. Remove the seeds and membranes with a spoon.

In a medium bowl, mix together the pepper jack cheese, cream cheese, garlic powder, onion powder, cumin, chili powder, salt, and black pepper until well combined.

Spoon the cheese mixture into each jalapeno half and press the halves back together.

In a shallow bowl, beat the egg. In another shallow bowl, add the panko bread crumbs.

Dip each jalapeno in the egg wash, then roll in the bread crumbs until coated.

Place the jalapenos on the prepared baking sheet and spray with cooking spray.

Bake for 20-25 minutes or until golden brown and crispy.

Serve hot with your favorite dipping sauce.

Enjoy your delicious Pepper Jack Cheese Jalapeno Poppers!

Eighteen

Potato Croquettes

Ingredients:

2 large potatoes, peeled and boiled
1/2 cup grated Parmesan cheese
1/4 cup chopped fresh parsley
1/4 teaspoon salt
1/4 teaspoon black pepper
1/4 teaspoon garlic powder
1/4 cup all-purpose flour
1 egg, beaten
1 cup breadcrumbs
Vegetable oil, for frying
Instructions:

Mash the boiled potatoes in a bowl and mix in the Parmesan cheese, parsley, salt, black pepper, and garlic powder.

Roll the mixture into small balls, about one inch in diameter.

Set up three bowls: one with flour, one with beaten egg, and one with breadcrumbs.

Roll each ball in flour, then dip in the egg, and coat with breadcrumbs.

Heat vegetable oil in a frying pan over medium-high heat.

Fry the croquettes until golden brown, about 2-3 minutes on each side.

Remove from the oil and place on paper towels to drain excess oil.

Serve warm with your favorite dipping sauce.

These potato croquettes are crispy on the outside and soft on the inside, making them the perfect appetizer for any occasion. Plus, the Parmesan cheese and parsley add a burst of flavor that will leave your guests wanting more. Enjoy!

Nineteen

Pickle-Stuffed Deviled Eggs

Ingredients:

6 large eggs
   2 tbsp mayonnaise
   1 tbsp dijon mustard
   1 tbsp pickle juice
   1/4 tsp salt
   1/4 tsp black pepper
   6 small pickles (gherkins), finely chopped
   Paprika, for garnish
   Instructions:

Hard boil the eggs by placing them in a pot, covering with cold water, and bringing to a boil. Once boiling, reduce the heat to low and simmer for 12 minutes. Drain and rinse with cold water before peeling.

Cut the eggs in half lengthwise and carefully remove the yolks. Place the yolks in a bowl and mash them with a fork.

Add the mayonnaise, dijon mustard, pickle juice, salt, and black pepper to the bowl with the yolks. Mix well until creamy.

Fold in the chopped pickles.

Spoon the mixture into the egg white halves and sprinkle with paprika.

Chill in the fridge for at least 30 minutes before serving.

These pickle-stuffed deviled eggs are a tangy twist on a classic appetizer that's sure to please any pickle-lover. Enjoy!

Twenty

Celery and Cream Cheese Stuffed Mini Peppers

Ingredients:

12 mini sweet peppers

4 oz cream cheese, softened

1/4 cup sour cream

1/4 cup chopped celery

1/4 tsp garlic powder

Salt and pepper to taste

Fresh parsley for garnish

Directions:

Preheat oven to 350°F (175°C).

Wash and dry the mini sweet peppers, and cut off the tops. Remove the seeds and membranes from inside.

In a medium bowl, mix together the cream cheese, sour cream, chopped celery, garlic powder, salt, and pepper.

Fill each pepper with the cream cheese mixture, using a spoon or a piping bag.

Arrange the peppers on a baking sheet lined with parchment paper.

Bake for 15-20 minutes, until the peppers are tender and the filling is golden brown.

Garnish with chopped parsley and serve warm.

This appetizer is perfect for parties or gatherings, and the combination of sweet peppers, creamy filling, and crunchy celery creates a delicious and memorable flavor.

Twenty-One

Salmon Cucumber Bites

Ingredients:
1 pound fresh salmon fillet, skin removed
1 large cucumber, sliced into rounds
1/4 cup Greek yogurt
1 tablespoon chopped fresh dill
1 teaspoon lemon juice
Salt and pepper to taste
Directions:
Preheat the oven to 400°F.

Cut the salmon into small pieces and season with salt and pepper.

Place the salmon on a baking sheet lined with parchment paper and bake for 10-12 minutes or until cooked through.

In a small bowl, mix together the Greek yogurt, dill, lemon juice, salt, and pepper.

Top each cucumber slice with a piece of cooked salmon and a dollop of the yogurt mixture.

Serve chilled and enjoy!

This recipe is perfect for a party or as a healthy snack. The combination of the juicy cucumber, flavorful salmon, and creamy yogurt mixture is sure to impress your guests. Plus, it's easy to make and can be prepared in advance.

Twenty-Two

Bruschetta with Tomato and Basil

Ingredients:

1 loaf of crusty Italian bread

4 large tomatoes, diced

1/4 cup fresh basil, chopped

2 cloves garlic, minced

3 tablespoons olive oil

Salt and pepper to taste

Instructions:

Preheat the oven to 375°F (190°C).

Slice the bread into 1/2-inch thick pieces and place them on a baking sheet.

In a small bowl, mix together the diced tomatoes, basil, garlic, olive oil, salt, and pepper.

Spoon the tomato mixture onto the bread slices, making sure to cover each piece evenly.

Bake the bruschetta in the oven for 10-12 minutes or

until the bread is golden brown and the tomatoes are slightly bubbly.

Remove from the oven and let cool for a few minutes.

Serve immediately and enjoy!

This appetizer is perfect for any occasion and is sure to impress your guests. The combination of fresh tomatoes, basil, and garlic on top of a crispy piece of bread is simply irresistible. Enjoy!

Twenty-Three

Black Bean and Corn Dip

Ingredients:

1 can of black beans, drained and rinsed
1 can of corn, drained
1 small red onion, finely chopped
1 small red bell pepper, finely chopped
1 jalapeño pepper, seeded and finely chopped
2 cloves garlic, minced
1/4 cup fresh cilantro, chopped
Juice of 1 lime
Salt and pepper to taste
Tortilla chips for serving
Instructions:

In a large bowl, combine the black beans, corn, red onion, red bell pepper, jalapeño pepper, garlic, and cilantro.

Add the lime juice and season with salt and pepper to taste.

Mix well and let the flavors meld in the refrigerator for at least 30 minutes before serving.

Serve with tortilla chips for dipping.

This dip is vegetarian, gluten-free, and full of flavor. The black beans and corn add a nice texture and protein to the dish, making it a satisfying and healthy appetizer option. Enjoy!

Twenty-Four

Tuna and Avocado Bites

Ingredients:

1 can of tuna, drained and flaked
1 ripe avocado, mashed
1 small red onion, finely chopped
2 tbsp cilantro, chopped
1 tbsp lime juice
Salt and pepper to taste
20-24 tortilla chips
Instructions:

In a medium bowl, mix together the tuna, mashed avocado, red onion, cilantro, lime juice, salt, and pepper.

Spoon a small amount of the tuna mixture onto each tortilla chip.

Serve chilled and enjoy!

These Tuna and Avocado Bites are a delicious and healthy appetizer that are perfect for any occasion. They're easy to make, and the combination of tuna and avocado is both re-freshing and satisfying. The cilantro and lime add a burst of flavor that really makes these bites stand out. Give them a try and see for yourself!

Twenty-Five

Almond-Crusted Goat Cheese Balls

Ingredients:

8 oz soft goat cheese
1/4 cup finely chopped almonds
1/4 cup panko breadcrumbs
1/4 tsp garlic powder
1/4 tsp dried thyme
1 egg, beaten
Olive oil for frying
Instructions:

In a small bowl, mix together the chopped almonds, panko breadcrumbs, garlic powder, and dried thyme.

Roll the goat cheese into small balls, about 1 inch in diameter.

Dip each ball into the beaten egg, then roll in the almond mixture to coat.

Heat a small amount of olive oil in a frying pan over medium heat.

Fry the goat cheese balls for about 2-3 minutes, turning until they are golden brown on all sides.

Remove from the pan and place on a paper towel to drain excess oil.

Serve warm with crackers or sliced baguette.

This appetizer recipe is perfect for any occasion. The crunchy almond coating gives the goat cheese balls a delicious texture and the herbs add a flavorful touch. Your guests will love this unique and tasty appetizer!

Twenty-Six

Paprika Spiced Sweet Potato Bites

Ingredients:

2 large sweet potatoes, peeled and diced into 1-inch cubes

2 tbsp olive oil

1 tsp smoked paprika

1 tsp garlic powder

1/2 tsp salt

1/4 tsp black pepper

1/4 cup sour cream

1 tbsp chopped fresh chives

Directions:

Preheat oven to 400°F.

In a large bowl, toss sweet potato cubes with olive oil, smoked paprika, garlic powder, salt, and black pepper.

Spread the sweet potato cubes evenly on a baking sheet.

Bake for 20 to 25 minutes, or until sweet potatoes are tender and lightly browned.

Remove from oven and let cool for a few minutes.

Serve warm with a dollop of sour cream and a sprinkle of chopped chives on top.

This appetizer is perfect for any occasion, and the combination of sweet potatoes and paprika is sure to be a crowd-pleaser. Enjoy!

Twenty-Seven

Spicy Onion Fritters

Ingredients:

2 cups finely chopped onions
  1/2 cup gram flour (chickpea flour)
  1/4 cup rice flour
  1/4 cup corn flour
  1 tsp red chili powder
  1/2 tsp turmeric powder
  1/2 tsp cumin powder
  1/2 tsp coriander powder
  Salt to taste
  Oil for deep frying
  Directions:

In a mixing bowl, combine the chopped onions, gram flour, rice flour, corn flour, red chili powder, turmeric powder, cumin powder, coriander powder, and salt.

Mix everything together well, then add enough water to form a thick batter.

Heat the oil in a deep frying pan.

When the oil is hot, take a spoonful of the onion batter and drop it into the oil.

Fry the fritters until they are golden brown and crispy.

Remove the fritters from the oil and drain them on a paper towel.

Serve the fritters hot with your favorite dipping sauce.

These spicy onion fritters are a perfect vegetarian appetizer that are easy to make and packed with flavor. The combination of the crunchy exterior and the soft, onion-filled interior will have your guests asking for seconds!

Twenty-Eight

Mediterranean Olive Bruschetta

Mediterranean Olive Bruschetta
Ingredients:

1 baguette, sliced
1/2 cup chopped Kalamata olives
1/2 cup chopped green olives
1/4 cup chopped sun-dried tomatoes
2 cloves garlic, minced
2 tablespoons chopped fresh basil
2 tablespoons chopped fresh parsley
1 tablespoon olive oil
Salt and pepper, to taste
Directions:

Preheat the oven to 375°F.

Arrange the baguette slices in a single layer on a baking sheet and bake for 5-7 minutes, or until lightly toasted.

In a medium bowl, combine the chopped Kalamata olives, green olives, sun-dried tomatoes, garlic, basil, parsley, olive oil, salt, and pepper.

Spoon the olive mixture onto the toasted baguette slices and serve.

This bruschetta is perfect for a Mediterranean-themed party or as a light summer appetizer. The combination of salty olives, tangy sun-dried tomatoes, and fresh herbs is sure to impress your guests. Enjoy!

Twenty-Nine

Sausage and Cheese Stuffed Mini Peppers

Ingredients:

12 mini peppers
1/2 pound sausage
1/2 cup shredded cheddar cheese
1/4 cup diced onion
1/4 cup diced bell pepper
1/4 cup diced celery
1/2 teaspoon garlic powder
Salt and pepper to taste
Instructions:

Preheat oven to 375°F.

Cut the tops off the mini peppers and scoop out the seeds.

In a skillet, cook the sausage over medium heat until browned. Drain any excess grease.

Add the onion, bell pepper, celery, garlic powder, salt, and pepper to the skillet and cook until vegetables are soft.

Remove skillet from heat and stir in the shredded cheese.

Stuff the sausage mixture into the mini peppers.

Place stuffed peppers on a baking sheet and bake for 15-20 minutes, or until peppers are tender and cheese is melted.

Serve warm and enjoy!

This appetizer is easy to make and is sure to please a crowd with its savory and cheesy flavors.

Thirty

Famous Deviled Eggs

Ingredients:

6 hard-boiled eggs
1/4 cup of mayonnaise
1 tablespoon of dijon mustard
1 tablespoon of sweet relish
1/4 teaspoon of garlic powder
Salt and pepper to taste
Paprika for garnish
Fresh parsley for garnish
Instructions:

Cut the hard-boiled eggs in half lengthwise and carefully remove the yolks.

In a small bowl, combine the egg yolks, mayonnaise, dijon mustard, sweet relish, and garlic powder. Mix well until smooth.

Season the mixture with salt and pepper to taste.

Spoon or pipe the mixture into the egg white halves.

Sprinkle paprika over the top of each egg for garnish.

Finally, add a small sprig of fresh parsley on top of each egg for an additional pop of color and flavor.

Enjoy your delicious and easy-to-make deviled eggs!

Thirty-One

Black Pepper and Parmesan Crusted Asparagus Appetizer

Ingredients:

1 bunch of asparagus, trimmed
1/4 cup of grated parmesan cheese
1/4 cup of breadcrumbs
1/2 teaspoon of black pepper
1/4 teaspoon of salt
1 egg, beaten
Cooking spray
Instructions:

Preheat your oven to 425°F (220°C).

In a small bowl, mix together the parmesan cheese, bread-crumbs, black pepper, and salt.

Dip each asparagus spear into the beaten egg, then coat them in the parmesan mixture.

Place the coated asparagus spears on a baking sheet coated with cooking spray.

Bake for 10-12 minutes or until the asparagus is tender and the coating is crispy.

Serve hot and enjoy!

This dish is perfect for any occasion, from dinner parties to casual get-togethers. The combination of black pepper and parmesan cheese creates a flavorful and savory crust that perfectly complements the asparagus.

Thirty-Two

Pan-Seared Scallops with Citrus Salsa

Ingredients:

12 large sea scallops, patted dry
1 tbsp olive oil
Salt and pepper, to taste
1 grapefruit, segmented and diced
1 orange, segmented and diced
1/2 small red onion, finely chopped
1 jalapeño pepper, seeded and finely chopped
1 tbsp honey
2 tbsp chopped fresh cilantro
Instructions:

In a mixing bowl, combine the grapefruit, orange, red onion, jalapeño pepper, honey, and cilantro to make the citrus salsa. Season with salt and pepper to taste.

Heat a large skillet over medium-high heat. Add the olive oil.

Season the scallops with salt and pepper. Add the scallops to the skillet and cook for 1-2 minutes per side, or until browned and cooked through.

Remove the scallops from the pan and set aside.

Spoon the citrus salsa onto a serving platter. Arrange the scallops on top of the salsa.

Serve immediately and enjoy!

This recipe is perfect for a light and refreshing appetizer that's easy to make and bursting with flavor. The sweetness of the scallops pairs perfectly with the tangy citrus salsa, and the jalapeño adds just the right amount of heat to balance out the dish. Give it a try and let me know what you think at waltertheeducator.com!

Thirty-Three

Cheddar Cheese and Bacon Stuffed Potato Skins

Ingredients:

4 large baking potatoes
6 strips of bacon
1 cup shredded cheddar cheese
2 tbsp chopped chives
1/4 cup sour cream
Salt and pepper to taste
Instructions:

Preheat oven to 400°F.

Wash potatoes and pierce each one a few times with a fork. Place the potatoes on a baking tray and bake for 1 hour or until tender.

While the potatoes are baking, cook the bacon in a skillet over medium heat until crispy. Once cooked, remove the bacon from the skillet and set aside on a paper towel to cool.

Once the potatoes are cooked, remove them from the oven and allow them to cool for a few minutes until they can be handled. Cut each potato in half lengthwise and scoop out the insides, leaving a thin layer of potato attached to the skin.

Chop the cooked bacon and mix it with the shredded cheddar cheese. Spoon the bacon and cheese mixture into the potato skins.

Return the stuffed potato skins to the oven and bake for an additional 10 minutes or until the cheese is melted and bubbly.

Remove the potato skins from the oven and sprinkle with chopped chives. Serve with a dollop of sour cream on top.

Enjoy your delicious appetizer of cheddar cheese and bacon stuffed potato skins!

Thirty-Four

Mini Quiches with Bacon and Cheddar Cheese

Ingredients:

1 1/2 cups all-purpose flour
1/2 tsp salt
1/4 tsp black pepper
1/2 cup unsalted butter, chilled and cubed
2 tbsp cold water
1/2 cup bacon, cooked and chopped
1/2 cup cheddar cheese, shredded
3 large eggs
1/2 cup heavy cream
1/4 tsp salt
1/4 tsp black pepper
Instructions:

Preheat the oven to 375°F.

In a large mixing bowl, whisk together flour, salt, and

pepper. Add butter and work with a pastry blender or your hands until the mixture becomes crumbly.

Add water and mix until the dough comes together.

Roll the dough out on a floured surface and cut small circles. Place the circles in a muffin tin and press the dough up the sides.

In a small bowl, mix together the bacon and cheddar cheese. Fill each muffin cup with a spoonful of the bacon and cheese mixture.

In a separate bowl, whisk together eggs, heavy cream, salt, and pepper.

Pour the egg mixture into each muffin cup until it is about 3/4 full.

Bake for 20-25 minutes or until the egg mixture is set and the crust is golden brown.

Serve warm and enjoy!

These mini quiches are easy to make and perfect for a party or gathering. They are sure to be a crowd-pleaser with their savory bacon and cheddar cheese filling and delicious crust.

Thirty-Five

Broccoli Cheddar Bites

Ingredients:

2 cups finely chopped broccoli
1 cup shredded cheddar cheese
1/2 cup panko breadcrumbs
1/4 cup grated Parmesan cheese
2 eggs
1/2 tsp garlic powder
Salt and pepper to taste
Instructions:

Preheat your oven to 375°F (190°C), and line a baking sheet with parchment paper.

In a mixing bowl, combine the chopped broccoli, cheddar cheese, panko breadcrumbs, Parmesan cheese, garlic powder, salt, and pepper.

In a separate bowl, beat the eggs.

Add the beaten eggs to the broccoli mixture, and stir until well combined.

Using a tablespoon or cookie scoop, form the mixture into small balls or patties, and place them on the prepared baking sheet.

Bake for about 20-25 minutes, or until golden brown and crispy on the outside.

Serve warm with your favorite dipping sauce.

Enjoy your delicious and healthy appetizer!

Thirty-Six

Tomato, Mozzarella, and Basil Crostini

Ingredients:

1 baguette, cut into thin slices
3 tbsp olive oil
2 garlic cloves, minced
1 cup cherry tomatoes, halved
8 oz fresh mozzarella cheese, sliced
1/4 cup fresh basil leaves, chopped
Salt and pepper, to taste
Instructions:

Preheat oven to 400°F.

In a small bowl, mix together the olive oil and minced garlic.

Brush each baguette slice with the garlic oil mixture and place on a baking sheet.

Bake for 5-7 minutes or until the bread is lightly toasted.

Remove from oven and top each slice with a slice of mozzarella cheese.

Return to the oven and bake for an additional 2-3 minutes or until the cheese is melted and bubbly.

Remove from oven and top each slice with halved cherry tomatoes.

Season with salt and pepper to taste.

Garnish with chopped fresh basil.

Serve warm and enjoy!

Thirty-Seven

Ham and Cheese Puff
Pastry Pinwheels

Ingredients:

1 sheet puff pastry, thawed
   4-5 slices of ham, chopped
   1/2 cup shredded cheddar cheese
   1 egg, beaten
   Salt & pepper to taste
   Instructions:

Preheat oven to 400°F.

On a lightly floured surface, roll out the puff pastry sheet into a rectangle.

In a small bowl, mix the chopped ham and shredded cheddar cheese.

Sprinkle the ham and cheese mixture over the puff pastry sheet.

Season with salt and pepper.

Roll the puff pastry tightly into a log shape.

Brush the beaten egg over the entire surface of the pastry log.

Cut the log into 1/2 inch slices and place them on a baking sheet lined with parchment paper.

Bake for 15-18 minutes, or until the pinwheels are golden brown and puffed up.

Serve warm and enjoy!

These Ham and Cheese Puff Pastry Pinwheels are sure to be a hit at any party or gathering. They're easy to make and taste absolutely delicious!

Thirty-Eight

Steak and Blue Cheese Crostini

Ingredients:

1/2 pound steak (sirloin or flank)
1 baguette, sliced into thin rounds
2 tablespoons olive oil
1/4 teaspoon garlic powder
Salt and pepper, to taste
1/4 cup crumbled blue cheese
1/4 cup chopped fresh parsley
Instructions:

Preheat oven to 400°F.

Brush the baguette slices with olive oil and sprinkle with garlic powder.

Place the slices on a baking sheet and bake for 6-8 minutes or until toasted.

Season the steak with salt and pepper on both sides.

Heat a skillet over high heat and add a tablespoon of olive oil.

Once the oil is hot, add the steak and cook for 3-4 minutes per side.

Remove the steak from the pan and let it rest for 5 minutes.

Once rested, slice the steak into thin strips.

Top each baguette slice with a strip of steak, crumbled blue cheese, and chopped parsley.

Serve immediately and enjoy!

This appetizer is perfect for any occasion, whether it's a fancy dinner party or a casual get-together with friends. The combination of juicy steak, tangy blue cheese, and fresh parsley on a crispy baguette slice is sure to impress your guests and leave them wanting more.

Thirty-Nine

Sweet and Sour Meatball Skewers

Ingredients:

1 pound ground beef
1/2 cup breadcrumbs
1/4 cup milk
1 egg
1/2 teaspoon onion powder
Salt and pepper to taste
1/2 cup ketchup
1/4 cup brown sugar
1/4 cup apple cider vinegar
1 tablespoon soy sauce
1/4 teaspoon garlic powder
1/4 teaspoon ginger powder
Wooden skewers
Instructions:
Preheat the oven to 375°F.

In a large bowl, mix together the ground beef, breadcrumbs, milk, egg, onion powder, salt, and pepper.

Roll the mixture into small meatballs, about 1 inch in diameter.

Place the meatballs on a baking sheet and bake for 15-20 minutes, or until cooked through.

While the meatballs are cooking, make the sweet and sour sauce. In a small saucepan, combine the ketchup, brown sugar, apple cider vinegar, soy sauce, garlic powder, and ginger powder. Cook over medium heat until the sugar has dissolved and the sauce has thickened, about 5 minutes.

Once the meatballs are done, remove them from the oven and let them cool slightly.

Thread 3-4 meatballs onto each wooden skewer.

Brush the sweet and sour sauce over the meatballs, making sure to coat them evenly.

Place the skewers back on the baking sheet and broil for 2-3 minutes, or until the sauce is bubbly and caramelized.

Serve the meatball skewers hot, with extra sweet and sour sauce on the side for dipping. Enjoy!

This recipe makes about 12 skewers, so it's perfect for a crowd. It's a sweet and savory appetizer that everyone will love.

Forty

Roasted Red Pepper and Feta Dip

Ingredients:

2 red peppers

    1/2 cup crumbled feta cheese

    1/4 cup plain Greek yogurt

    1 garlic clove, minced

    2 tablespoons chopped fresh parsley

    Salt and pepper to taste

    Pita chips or sliced vegetables for serving

    Instructions:

Preheat the oven to 450°F.

Cut the red peppers in half and remove the seeds and stems.

Place the peppers cut side down on a baking sheet lined with parchment paper.

Roast the peppers in the oven until the skin is charred and blistered, about 20-25 minutes.

Remove the peppers from the oven and let them cool. Once cooled, remove the skin and chop the flesh.

In a medium bowl, mix together the chopped peppers, feta cheese, Greek yogurt, garlic, parsley, salt, and pepper.

Serve the dip with pita chips or sliced vegetables.

This dip is creamy, tangy, and full of flavor. It's perfect for parties, gatherings, or just as a snack. Enjoy!

Walter the Educator is one of the pseudonyms for Walter Anderson. Formally educated in Chemistry, Business, and Education, he is an educator, an author, a diverse entrepreneur, and the son of a disabled war veteran. "Walter the Educator" shares his time between educating and creating. He holds interests and owns several creative projects that entertain, enlighten, enhance, and educate, hoping to inspire and motivate you.

WaltertheEducator.com